TREAT TOO!

TWO TAILS ARE BETTER THAN ONE

CHRISTIAN VIELER

BLACK DOG
& LEVENTHAL
PUBLISHERS
NEW YORK

Black Dog & Leventhal Publishers
Hachette Book Group
1290 Avenue of the Americas
New York, NY 10104

www.hachettebookgroup.com
www.blackdogandleventhal.com

First Edition: August 2021

Black Dog & Leventhal Publishers is an imprint of Perseus Books, LLC, a subsidiary of Hachette Book Group, Inc. The Black Dog & Leventhal Publishers name and logo are trademarks of Hachette Book Group, Inc.

The publisher is not responsible for websites (or their content) that are not owned by the publisher.

The Hachette Speakers Bureau provides a wide range of authors for speaking events. To find out more, go to www.HachetteSpeakersBureau.com or call (866) 376-6591.

Print book interior design by Katie Benezra

ISBNs: 978-0-7624-7238-3 (hardcover), 978-0-7624-7237-6 (ebook)

Printed in China

APS

10 9 8 7 6 5 4 3 2 1

I DEDICATE THIS BOOK TO MY FAMILY.

Thank you, Mom, for your neverending support.

Thank you, Linda & Tamml, Lotte, Anni, and Alfred,
who are always at my side. Cheers.

INTRODUCTION

Toward the end of 2015, an image agency approached me about my photographs, which, up to that point, had only been in photography forums like 500px. Just a few days later, my work was everywhere—including some of the most renowned newspapers in the world—and quickly went viral online. It was unbelievable. Within hours, an avalanche of social media developed, which quickly overran my entire life. What started as a living room hobby developed rapidly during perhaps the most exciting time of my life. There were television appearances, interviews, and an everyday life that I was suddenly able to dedicate entirely to dogs and photography. Plus, I published my first book, *Treat!*, which still makes me proud today.

Now you have *Treat Too!* in your hands and may be wondering whether to buy the book or not. With all my heart I can only say, "Yes—do it." I am not saying this because you should finance my dream car for me or convince my publisher to sign up *Treat Three!* Because, really, what's better than one dog? How about two or even three? All of the photographs in this book show two or three dogs snapping for that much-sought-after treat. Besides the pure joy, anticipation, and sometimes concern of a single dog vying for a tasty morsel, there is now an added level of competition. You can almost see exclamations like, "Hey, what are you doing?" or, "But no I first!" or, "Attention, clear the way!" on the pups' faces.

Just like *Treat!*, *Treat Too!* simply warms the heart. I've had such a wonderful time photographing these special dogs and hope that they add a similar joy to your lives.

Yours,
Christian Vieler

Note: All dog pairs have been carefully selected. The depicted animals often live in the same household or have known each other for many years. Please do not try to take similar pictures with unknown dogs.

DOG INDEX

Lilly and Chicko, Labradors

Nala and Kurt, long-haired
Chihuahua and Border collie

Louie and Lila,
Brittany spaniel and Labrador

Debbie and Quincy, basset hounds

Pebbles and Ninchi,
mini Australian shepherds

Balou and Pepe, Border collie mix
and mixed breed

Nele and Amy, Labradors

Lotta and Laila, Havaneses

Lennox and Skyy, Malinois

Dushi and Pepper, Labrador–Australian shepherd mix and Australian shepherd

Nika and Milo, French bulldogs

Damian and Lilly, Australian shepherd–golden retriever mixes

Fila and Riva, golden retrievers

Fibi and Tara, poodles

Selma and Marla, mixed breed and Labrador

Tamml and Lotte, mixed breed and Labrador

Milo and Melly, Australian shepherds

Sookie and Smilla, Boston terriers

Bazula and Bella, French bulldogs

Hilda and Hedwig, Cardigan Welsh corgis

Nele and Amy, Labradors

Ben and Louis, vizslas

Boyka and Dea, cane corsos

Barney and Floyd, mixed breeds

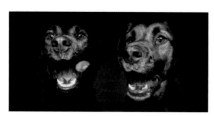

Moritz and Aika, Border collie
and Australian shepherd mix

Bella and Emma, boxers

Ben and Lilly, golden retrievers

A'Sita and Nero, Malinois and Doberman

Anton and Manfred, French bulldogs

Amy and Ole, Border collie mix
and Australian shepherd

Tenya and Mr. Crumble,
American bulldogs

Fiete and Pandora,
Jack Russell terrier and bichon

Nala and Kurt, Long-haired Chihuahua
and Border collie

Amy and Rose,
toy fox terrier and Border collie

Pitt and Nale, toy terrier and Chihuahua

Lola and Lilly, poodles

Addi and Hupe, Jack Russell terriers

Liese and Lotte, Australian shepherds

Mila and Lee, miniature pinschers

Mila and Milo, Australian shepherds

Pia and Mila, mixed breeds

Frieda and Bailey,
Labrador and white Swiss shepherd

Suki and Suko,
Border collie mix and Spitz mix

Qullny and Rosie, Cardigan Welsh corgis

Kuma and Danu, Alaskan malamute
and Siberian husky

Diego and Jette, mixed breeds

Alice and Elo, Akita–Chow mix
and West Highland terrier

Filou and Hugo, pugs

Nika and Mylo, French bulldogs

Amy and Ayu, Australian shepherd
and Weimaraner

Anni and George, boxer–pit bull mix
and French bulldog

Mila and Lee, miniature pinschers

Schorsch and Soey, American bulldogs

Donna and Frida, Rhodesian ridgebacks

Honey and Maya, Australian shepherds

Anni and Lotte,
Doberman and Labrador

Lina and Karlo, boxers

Chuna and Mojo, mixed breeds

Didi and Maja, mixed breeds

Ben and Lilly, golden retrievers

Vinur and Glenn, Icelandic sheepdog
and Border collie–Australian shepherd mix

Janosch and Leika, mixed breeds
Marty McFly and Nikita vom Schwarzen

See, Elo-cattle dog mix and Elo

Sally and Flocke, white Swiss shepherd
and German shepherd

Lotte and Laska, Labrador and
mixed breed

Honey and Maya, Australian shepherds

Anton and Mino, golden retrievers

James and Nedd, golden retrievers

Findus and Sweety, mixed breeds